(T)RAVEL/UN(T)RAVEL

For Janet—

To an accomplished poet who
no longer needs serial workshops!
You're a teacher ___

(T)RAVEL /
UN(T)RAVEL

Poems

NEIL SHEPARD

Neil Shepard

05/24/2012

MID-LIST PRESS
Minneapolis

Published by Mid-List Press. Visit our Web site at www.midlist.org.

Mid-List Press publishes books of high literary merit and fresh artistic vision by new and emerging writers and by writers ignored, marginalized, or excluded from publication by commercial and mainstream publishers. Mid-List seeks to increase access to publication for new writers, to nurture the growth of emerging writers, and, generally, to increase the diversity of books, authors, and readers. Mid-List Press is a tax-exempt, 501(c)(3), not-for-profit literary organization.

The poems listed below have been published in the following literary magazines: *ACM (Another Chicago Magazine)*, "Monkey Forest Road"; *Colorado Review*, "Pont de L'Alma, Looking Back at Sacre Coeur," "Whitby Abbey"; *Harvard Review*, "Physician in the Dark"; *The Journal*, "Aubade, West of Paris (early spring)"; *New American Writing*, "C'est Dommage"; *New Ohio Review*, "Travel: Choler"; *North American Review*, "Pleasant Weather in Cornwall"; *Notre Dame Review*, "Benedictine Abbey," "The Ancient Walls of San Gusme," "Siena," "If I Have to Die, and I Have to"; *Saranac Review*, "Blue Banlieue," "Gray Banlieue"; *Shenandoah*, "Giverny"; *Southern Poetry Review*, "(T)ravel/Un(T)ravel," "Punting on the Cam"; *Southwest Review*, "Snowdon Philosophy"; *TriQuarterly*, "Vincent, at Saint Remy Sanitarium"; *Western Humanities Review*, "Wuyi Mountain Cave." The following poems, reprinted from *I'm Here Because I Lost My Way* (Mid-List Press, 1998) and *This Far from the Source* (Mid-List Press, 2006) were originally published in these magazines: *Chariton Review*, "Ghost Talk"; *New England Review*, "Corfu"; *Spoon River Poetry Review*, "Equator Daze"; *Western Humanities Review*, "Lush Life."

Cover Art: *Coaster* by Beth Dow. Copyright © 2011 Beth Dow. Used by permission. (www.bethdow.com)

Cover and text design: Lane Stiles

Library of Congress Cataloging-in-Publication Data
Shepard, Neil, 1951–
  (T)ravel—un(t)ravel : poems / Neil Shepard.
    p. cm.
  Includes bibliographical references.
  ISBN 978-0-922811-88-5 (trade pbk. : alk. paper)
  I. Title.
  PS3569.H39395T63 2011
  811'.54—dc23
                              2011041011

CONTENTS

For Kate, my companion in love and travel

In some ways, modern American literary history can be seen as an unresolvable dialectic between regionalism and internationalism, as two competing identities for the writer.

Dana Gioia, from "Historical and Critical Overview,"
Twentieth Century American Poetry

(T)RAVEL/UN(T)RAVEL

You've met them, travelers half-
returned from afar, curled on a couch, comfortable,

uncomfortable, worrying gifts from elsewhere—
a tattooed cow skull, a friend's gamelan inlaid with bone

and pearl, a chipped tiki from a tohua.
You've seen them unravel as the other world

spins into view. Perhaps you've felt the vertigo, too—

the pig's throat slit, spit dripped in a kava bowl,
maggots in a plate of noodles, squid's eye

stabbed with a heke stick, its inky signature
floating across the coral reef—

How well you know the abrupt dislocation of matter—
firewalkers in Fiji, blue glaciers in Norway.

Eyes squinting in Tahitian sun,
wide open over Mongolian grassland,

your gaze the rose windows at Chartres,
the glazed mosaics of the Alhambra,

your ear the growing comprehension
of Shanghai slang, flamenco shout, Marquesan pig-grunt,

your hand gesturing toward the street, the sea, the rim
of horizon, a white flash of surrender . . .

ONE

America is to be kept coarse and broad . . . The air here is very strong. Much that stands well and has a little enough place provided for it in the small scales of European kingdoms and empires, here stands haggard, dwarfed, ludicrous.

> Walt Whitman
> from "Letter to Ralph Waldo Emerson,"
> included in the 2nd edition of *Leaves of Grass*

Not that Americans today can be anything less than citizens of the world; but being inclined to run off to London and Paris it is inexplicable that in every case they have forgotten or not known that the experience of native local contacts, which they take with them, is the only thing that can give that differentiated quality of presentation to their work which at first enriches their new sphere and later alone might carry them far as creative artists in the continental hurly-burly.

> William Carlos Williams
> from "Yours, O Youth"

(T)RAVEL/UN(T)RAVEL: MONKEY FOREST ROAD (Ubud, Bali)
for William Carlos Williams

Pinned under mesh netting, I awake
to mosquitoes and geckoes, brash anjing
howling outside, fighting cocks bruising

the air. The market's squawk is a block off,
where women smelling of raw fish, their breasts
burst from their shirts, and men hawking

and emptying their nostrils on the sidewalks,
shout *Mister, mister!* This morning I can
roll over and refuse it—the Balinese

begging *Buy ticket to Kechak monkey
dance, buy wood carving of garuda—*
refuse, roll over, and burrow deeper

into my wife's awakening flesh, into
the blond texture of her hair. Or I can
attend today's dance of Ramayana where women

with pitch dark hair twisted back along their necks
will imitate the flight of blue herons,
where men chattering *chak chak chak* will ape

a troop of monkeys, while the gamelan
players hammer hypnotic fire trance scales.
I can refuse it all—the toothless woman

who drapes her stained sarong around my waist
and hisses *sixty rupiah,* the scarred guard
blocking entrance to Monkey Forest:

Five hundred rupiah, he says, and snatches
it away. Or guards at the Floating Palace
who forbid me to enter the puri

without the dignity of bare feet
and spirit, dressed in sarong and sash.
I can refuse even the holy men

of the island who subsist on sunlight
and quiet, teaching the body bathed
in sensation that being blinds us,

distracts us from the world behind the world.
The sun won't clarify this hazy morning.
Which is why I will arise, finally,

from this twisted, simian knot, and climb
to a higher brain asking, How will I meet
those black eyes begging *Mister, mister.*

How will I descend the steps to Gulung Kawi
where secret burial chambers of the monks
have been laid bare—labyrinths of honey-

combed sarcophagi, corridors of deep quiet
dug down through sandstone, down under the rice
terraces, the hand dug canals, down to deep

rivers carrying the rainy season away.
How will I arrive there unscathed and prepared?
Or will I always arrive scarred and fearful,

my meditations unravelling.
And will I always succumb to the man
with the machete who stirs his hands

through my prayers as through muddied water
and says, *Mister, buy my coconut.*
Out the door, down into the streets with you—

lost in the funeral dance on Monkey Forest Road.

SQUARE VIVANI

Always, the dizzied tourists with *Green Guides* and blue maps tumbling open, looking up to the glinting spires and domes, down to the merde-brown Seine; frocked priests and habited nuns hidden in long black hot robes; short-skirted mothers with jog-strollers; and sleeveless-chemise youth leaning back on green benches somewhere in the middle of torpor-inducing kisses, long soporific kisses in which two lovers melt into one mouth, one hunger, one springtime, under the newly leaved plane trees.

How chopped they seemed all winter, impossible to recover. Out of season, their mouths were buried under knotted scarves, their kisses bruised behind high doors. The filthy ones, unhoused, unhouselled, slept on metal benches in the Underground. An empty wheelchair beside the Seine. A body stiff beside the ruined stones of Eglise de St. Julien le Pauvre. But here they are just past Easter, green shade in abundance from winter surgery, lovers lounging on green benches, the homeless stretching on patches of grass. Now all the mouths yawn open for air, taking it even from other mouths, other lungs. After the long-held winter breath, everybody breathes. Everybody wakes together.

AUBADE, WEST OF PARIS
(early spring)

throw open the doors—

almonds flowering
snow on trees, plums purpling
the black limbs of winter

flowering—the *ing* is the thing
zing!—dang if I ain't plain *tame*
this morning. I been dead
all winter, so tame is *wild!*
where I come from.

daffodils are yellow, not yellowed—
kids disappear in forsythia—
guardians on high alert, floating
over trees disguised as pink clouds—

throw open the doors!—

burble like a fool—you've bungled enough
years—burble, bungle, to hell
with the middle way, temper-
ance is our condition,
more than we admit—not enough
heart epaulets—not after thirty, no—

hereby decree all public men and women
shall sew hearts on sleeves or else—
shipped off to flower factories—

rough winds do shake
the darling buds—how long
can these little courage-makers hang on?

CORFU

Late afternoon we watch the waters change—
aquamarine, cerulean, royal blue, blue-violet.
And now, violet, deep violet. And now black.

The patio lights say your eyes are blue, your lids
purple, your skin copper. The glow of Greek morning's
still upon your face. And what came later—

something far from the jeweled coastlines
and secret coves where lovers dive, make love,
preserve each others' bodies with sun-oils.

Somewhere far into the interior of the island
where groves of orange, lemon, lime, shiver
in heat, where fragrant myrrh and olive

mask a far older smell. All comes back to us
this evening in the sweep of mountain wind.
We feel a certain nakedness remembering

the backfire of our mopeds on the mountain
road, young fruit-pickers perched in the foliage,
their heads emerging like globed fruits as we passed.

Arriving in a white-washed village,
we blew black smoke in siesta-sun,
until the children pegged pebbles, pointing

and running and begging. Women's black-veiled heads hung
out their windows, and their bony fingers pointed.
Town-fathers plied us with ouzo, retsina,

then wrapped their legs around us in an old
Ionian dance, and their hunger drove us
farther out on the mountain road where blind

beggar-widows huddle in their black shawls.
As we sputtered and belched black fumes, they caught us
in the cross hairs of their eyeless stares, worse than

the eye of the all-knowing, two black holes for sockets,
and the leprous nose, and that last hole
of darkness where the mouth opens in need,

the language foreign but familiar to any traveler.
Tonight we still see them as the Corfu waters
go violet, go black. Hands rise from scaly limbs

and they beg with their missing fingers.

FROM PONT DE L'ALMA, LOOKING BACK AT SACRÉ COEUR ON MONTMARTRE

Just before you cross the bridge to Pont de l'Alma,
look back—over your left shoulder—the way Orpheus
sought Eurydice or Lot's wife sought a last salty taste
of Sodom. Unlike Orpheus, you'll see the shimmering form
of the Sacré Coeur, if you're lucky, backlit by clouds, as if
it were floating, detached from horizon, ready to join you
wherever you walk. Unlike Lot's wife, you'll have a name
and an avenue-guided view of those salt-white domes.
No god will block your lusty gaze with a petrifying white-out.
You'll have as long as you desire to drink in its shape and shimmer
before you're drunk with this-worldliness or other-worldliness
or plain remorse: the closer you come to those stiff pillars,
the farther off the soft, amorphous clouds recede. You're better off,
perhaps, to let that last vision shimmer at your shoulder, always visible,
always unattainable, like Christ walking beside you on the road to Emmaus,
like the Angel of Mercy, her finger stretched to tap your left shoulder, should you
forget the soft contours of life. Forget what's important in your long walks along the avenues.
And that is? That's none of your business. Just as you'll never know the last thoughts
of any common criminal on his way to the gallows, guillotine, firing squad, electric chair,
who turns back a last time to his executioners, or beyond them, to the world
he never made but always wanted, the world always beyond him, that made him
commit the first crime, and the next, and the one after that, until his unbearable
heart led him here, without remorse, thirsting, dry-eyed, still licking his salt-wounds.

I SAY NADA TO NADA
    (Cadiz, Spain)

OK. Let's get Hemingway out of the way right away.
    Here's the gun. Goodbye. De nada.

Now let's get on with the main subject—
    back when there was a subject. Nada.

Thirty-three years ago in Cadiz, I lost
    myself to nada—and who hasn't?

or else—how has one lived?—lost
    my rude tongue, my identifying swagger, my famous

self-possession—all falsified and forfeited
    in a series of drunken, deteriorating days veering

toward nada. So what, you say? OK, here's the gun.
    I was twenty, ripped jeans, rucksack, cervezas and chasers.

I was dinner at 5 o'clock, no entiendo to every god-
    damn thing. I was guidebook-challenged. OK, cock it.

I slept on a Eurail pass. Wandered the cobblestones muttering
    my one line, ¿Dónde está barato pensión?

Lost my lunch on a slow-train sour with goats and chicken-shit.
    Don't I sound like everyone else? Like nada?

OK, uncock it. Point it: thirty-three years later—that's how long
    Christ wandered this dustball before he choked on it—

And though I suffered my own El Greco scenes, it was nada
    compared to Jésu's solo journey. No, I found other loves—

many who washed my tired feet at night—then lashed them
    to my street-shoes in the morning.

12

What I'm saying is nada hid in the smell
          of my socks, laundry lint in my bellybutton,

in the husks of marriage rice, in the umbilicus sliced away
          from my daughter as she squeezed toward the light.

Now I'm solidly en familia, mi muchacha y mi mujer holding me up, holding
          me back, if I move too fast toward the hookah tables.

I've progressed—is what I'm saying—toward *somethingness,*
          toward those slow talkers inside me who cock their heads

and give me that I'll-be-here-a-while look—but different
          than the old glazed stares in the bars. The old nada.

The other side of en familia? The sock-smell, lint-dust, still linger
          every day. And other identities go hungry.

But here in Cadiz, I line them up side by side at the tapas bars.
          And they talk it out, under the thousand-year-old olive trees,

great-grandsires of trees planted by the Phoenicians, those first wanderers,
          who rode the swelling nothingness of the sea

and settled, finally, on this solid, sea-lashed piece of land.

I am certain of nothing but of the holiness of the Heart's affections.
—Keats's letter to Benjamin Bailey

KEATS HOUSE, HAMPSTEAD HEATH

Spring insists on these pink flowers loaded with nectar-obsessed bees—
not the drowsy sounds of nightingales you heard under plum boughs,
not the clammy cells of autumn bees. *Nectar:* "to get over death."
Lift *glum* up from his supine pose on the "Sopha bed" and lead him
to the scented garden. As when Fanny breathed beyond the lavender
wall and you alive on the other side began to stir to her scent,
felt the paper-thin cell that held you apart begin to vibrate,
both of you humming up and down your lengths the first honeyed measures
that would take you through a year—spring's green heath, summer's swimming ponds,
before the sphagnum bog browned and arterial blood coughed up from a lung
deposited its bright death warrant on your handkerchief in mid-winter,
sent you southward to your name writ with water. Hold the nectar
in your hands today—wisteria purples the canopy over the walkway,
no wistfulness in the air. Tom's death, Fanny's distance, Charles's departure
after you grew too weak to ramble the hills with him—suspend it
on a bough, on a painted urn, in an eager breeziness the bees possess
when they're sticky with honey. If Fanny asks for a love-courtesy
that lasts forever—say *yes*.

ROT AND BLOSSOM
        for Walt Whitman

Those days in Shanghai we were in love
with the nighest scent of rot and blossom
on Guangling Yi Lu, wandering the market street
where butchers cleaved chicken heads, pigs feet,
pulled fish from plastic tubs, hacked
off their heads, or whacked them with the flat
of the cleaver until they trembled and lay still,
then wrapped them in the Chinese news,
long on distortion, short on revelation.

Sometimes, when the smell of thousand-year-old
eggs and rotting duck overcame us, or sometimes,
when Shanghai slang and formal Han muddled
our heads, we'd retreat to the foreigner's compound
to soak in the cadences of English, retreat further
to the bedroom—but the smells would follow us in—
hot pepper oil and sizzling garlic mixing
with the salt odor of sex and the sweet honey
on our legs that dried and clung like a second skin.

Back and forth, back and forth—to the street's
vegetable vendors washing night soil from tomatoes,
men grinding scythed wheat, women pulling strands
of wheat dough into long noodles, men hammering
tin into pots and kettles, women patching flat tires
of bicycles as the riders held them between their legs,
and one roadside dentist yanked a rotted tooth from the black hole
of a woman's mouth, right there on the sidewalk, the patient spitting
a bright spray of blood into the street.

And back to bed where, those days, we made love
against the martial music blaring beyond our window,
the CP cadres ordering a regime of good health
for their citizens three times a day: once during the eight-count
morning exercises—*yi, er, san, si, wu, liu, chi, ba*—loudspeaker
broadcasts from every park and market, every nursery and university
in our square block of ten thousand workers and students,
most of them, on the verge of turning regimen
to riot, to payback for the massacre at Tiananmen—

but for now, they flung their arms skyward and sliced
the air, they pushed their bodies up from the dirt,
they ran in place. On their own time, they practiced
Falung Gung's spirit-power, or followed Fu Liang,
the Allen Ginsberg of China, prophesying to his audience:
My fingers are ten robust candles that could flame up
They will burn up the whole curtain of night
They will rearrange the shapeless, twisted streets and lanes
Everything will be more open and spirited than strong sunlight.

And once before chi fan, the shared lunch, when the noon hour
filled with torpor and oral sex, shellfish warm and bloating
in the sun, worms wriggling in bowls of noodles, and after sex,
looking out the window to a taxi driver's slumped form snoozing
over the steering wheel, or another's lean, luxurious recline,
his head resting on the rubber of the opened window, his exquisitely
long pinky nail picking bloody scabs out of his nose,
and the many silky, black-haired others stumbling by,
shouting and laughing and spitting in the street.

And once in the evening, the patriotic music stiff and tinny –
erased, utterly, by the sound of an er hu from our quad, its gut-
wrenching one string bending music to querulous interrogatives,
rising up from a street-level apartment—*whither the future*
of China, in spirit, or matter?—and a listless answer,
a simple bamboo flute, the music floating down

from the rooftop where someone played, where caged
pigeons made their guttural calls and caged
crickets scraped their songs in early evening.

Far off, we could see the lurid red and blue billboards pulsing
along the Bund, Mao's red star shimmering over the newest high-rise,
the Bank of China, the currency of yuan and remnimbi, rising, slowly rising.
We could almost feel the spirit-power of these bustling roadside markets changing
into wads of US dollars, British pounds—almost see the future
of the Bund's right bank, rows of hovels bulldozed
for the square acres of skyscrapers to come; the million
bicycles confiscated or relegated to narrow lanes, making way
for the corps of Mercedes and Volvos to come; the white-masked

street sweepers, with their straw brooms and iron rice bowls, replaced
by early-morning water trucks hosing down the streets; the oil refinery clouds
on the outskirts of Shanghai become a permanent gray residue over the city.
But we turned back to bed, back to the spicy, seductive smells
of the market still mixed in our sheets, and traded a few Chinese curses
or blessings: *May you live in interesting times. May a thousand flowers bloom . . .*

TWO

While this America settles in the mould of its vulgarity, heavily thickening to empire,
And protest, only a bubble in the molten mass, pops and sighs out, and the mass hardens,
I sadly smiling remember that the flower fades to make fruit, the fruit rots to make earth.

Robinson Jeffers
from "Shine, Perishing Republic"

(T)RAVEL/ UN(T)RAVEL: CHOLER
for Robinson Jeffers

We had come to the Great Wall's end
in the desert of Jiaguyuan. Our tempers flared
across the crumbled battlements, out into the red heat.
There were weeds, thorns, a few hard-
shelled bugs. Love reduced to a black
carapace, under which a stinger,
a biting mouth, a reflex, a poison.

Heat withered our patience. Our bowels,
stung by a virus, made us say words we'd regret—
peevish, pernicious—*wo yao, wo yao,*
I want, I want, and nothing else.
We both stormed off—"stormed"
could have brought some moisture
to this desert, but no, this storm

was a hot wind, stinging sand
in the face, chipped sandstone
from the last outpost, that would cut
and bury us. Wei guoren. Barbarian.

Stripped of camouflage, of greenery, fluidity,
we showed every tic and flaw.

I could not stand one more day of mei you—
Not have. Not possible. Not ever.
I could not stand in one more ticket line,
elbowed, elbowing for a hard-sleeper berth
out of the heat. *Come back tomorrow.*
Tomorrow and tomorrow . . . stretching away
like the Great Wall disappearing into red dust.

There was a Hami melon, the best
melon in the desert, it was said,

pale green rind, and inside
a thick, luscious yellow.
Mei you to melons, to Hami, to anything
but a few dry husks in the streets
where others had stood, ticketless, for days.

I could have spit in any traveler's face.
I could have spit in her face, and she in mine.
I could have spit in the wind and hit myself and liked it.
I could have tasted black bile in every phlegmy word launched against the dryness.

Down beneath the desert in a crypt, I saw
an ancient face, preserved in this dry heat, shrunk
to a withered visage, devoid of the good
wetness that waters our lips with thanks,
its lips turned down in an arid scowl
for four thousand years.

MARQUESAS

Matins, and the village Marias
lead me to the water's edge

where squid hide in coral mounds.
Spears and a true aim.

We stab the eye, pluck out
the ink sack. Watch its final signature

written purple across the coral reef.

       •

Vespers, and the village boys
lead me to the jungle's edge

where hens roost in the trees.
Flashlights and bamboo poles.

We tip them from their limbs.
One free-

falling moment, one weak cluck,
and the abrupt neck-snap.

       •

Lately, as I gather the fallen
guava, grapefruit, tangerine,

I imagine meat beneath a chicken's wing.
And lately, as I climb toward the high

limbs of orange, mango, corasol,
I see a spear through the under-

belly of a fairy tern. How easy
to pluck it from this in-

carnation to bloom on a dinner plate.

·

Wind snaps the stem that binds
fruit to limb.

Wind cuts through us
as we turn

from fruit to game.
We walk into the wind

that carries their scent—
wild goat or pig or steer.

Two hunting dogs and a knife
through the wind-

pipe bring down a pig.
One dog alone kills a kid

and sends its mother bounding.
The steer's another matter.

·

Well past complin, wind whips
through Anaho Pass where tattooed

hunters lead me to the high plains.
There the steers doze.

I join two Marquesans
who come between the horns

of startled bulls and plunge
their machetes home.

•

Tomorrow, we'll climb down
for the feast of saints.

Tomorrow, we'll pray to the coral
Mary on the mountaintop

who casts her shadow
across this valley,

who blesses sacrifice—fruit,
fowl, fish, and flesh.

FOLLOWING IN THE FOOTSTEPS OF MELVILLE

Mostly, he sat on his fat ass
and spun a sea-faring yarn
while Fayaway wove white tappa,

Kori-Kori fetched his pipe
and together they taught him
the ancient names of things.

These days, Marquesans have a name
for men like him: haoie tivava
(white liars). Those who steal

a song, a story from the heart
of things, who leave little in return.
And I'm another, I claim good company:

Melville, Gauguin, Stevenson,
London, Brel, Brookes, and a hundred
more rovers from Suggs to Theroux.

I teach English in the mornings,
write their lives into poems all afternoon,
and learn their songs by evening.

I have a wife, thus no Fayaway.
I own no pipe. I even help
two old ones—two Typee, as Melville

used to say—roll their own smokes,
two dozer men razing old
tohua stones to raise a church –

both drunk on sabbath morning,
as is the custom after custom
has been washed away—not by booze

but by waves of haoies—after
ancient memory has dried up
and mind is a parched landscape.

Then the thirst comes on. *Haoies!*
yells one dozer man when he sees
us. *Tivava!* when he learns

my wife's an anthropologist,
professional apologist
for haoie's sins. You're here to steal

what's left of our memory.
You'll write a book. *Make money,*
Make money. That's all a haoie

knows. Some of us still know
the ancient tongue—he slurs
through a beer haze. Some still know

the fathers of fathers of fathers
who knew that liar, Melville.
He called us lazy, but where

did our plenty come from?
Only in dreams does everything
grow on trees. He mocked our tongue,

but gibberish is wax
in a conqueror's ears.
Savages, he called us. Who savaged

our lands, our memories?
Who came bearing gifts and syphilis,
doctors and smallpox, missions

and omissions such as
the general provisions of
paradise and hell. Now we

know it well: *Make money, make
money. That's all a haoie knows.*
Now jungles swallow our tohua stones,

old dance sites and prayer pits.
We're left with absence, silence.
Our lives turned to profit, to live

forever in your books or in
the vacuum-weather of museums.
Make money, Make money.

That's all a haoie knows.

HADRIAN'S WALL

Another ditch, another mound, another Roman mile
over Whin Sill, over ridges of basalt and heather
before two turrets and one chester are raised
from rubble and stone—all hauled on these large
carts, by horse and by human, from one mile or from eighty.
And all because the Emperor has willed it, Hadrian,
who has himself come to these wild lands where Picts swarm
like midges and seem to rise out of every crag and tor
to thwart us. Our master builders say six years, at least,
before the wall is sealed—six years before I smell again
the perfumed girls of the market square. No aqueduct or Roman road
will have required more of us. And continue to require.
Two turrets and one chester. Five guards for each turret set
on a barren, windy site, and one legion for each chester—
five hundred foot soldiers and two hundred horsemen—
to gather our forces in one fort for each mile across the neck
of Britain until it is broken. A hundred thousand soldiers
honored, or rotting, here on the Borderlands between Rome's light
and Pictish darkness. And all because Hadrian wills it. But I have heard
how barely three hundred years ago, the Yellow Emperor ordered
China's Great Wall to rise, and still, Mongolian hordes
breeched it. Or rather, bribed guards to pass through.
Well, we will remain steadfast, and honorable.
But I would wish a place at a turret outpost, where honor
means facing a month of wind, white crags, purple heather,
and few men to listen to my thoughts. They are dark as the violent
sky, lonely as the betrayed, blank as the rolling moors where Picts kneel
in their caves and sharpen their pikes—their one thought, to have a Roman
heart dangling at the end of each spear, to go to our graves heartless.

THE ANCIENT WALLS OF SAN GUSME

Why is it, in the little town of San Gusme,
amidst the clatter of dinnerware and clink of chianti bottles,
amidst the heavy laughter and gruff oaths and loud
overtures and postures of Italian lawyers at law,
when one man scraped back his chair, arose,
and clicked over the clay tiles to the grand
piano, the room already began to hold its breath,
and when he played a schmaltzy popular tune
just well enough for us to recognize it, still
it quieted us, and reminded us of the quiet
outside, the off-season cobblestone,
the medieval walls close around us
and what they were for, and another loudness
that had saltpeter and blood in it, and though
the tune was only competent, it was good enough
to remind us where we were, how far we'd come,
how far we could fall, in a loud unmindful instant.

•

Then one lawyer said he could see in my face
I was "Yiddish." He could see I was "an artist"
and "artists have suffered." I liked him very much for this,
didn't like him for that. When I played on the piano
a jazzy version of "Rock of Ages," his table applauded.
Then he stood, uninvited, made a formal speech
about we Americans, about the Yiddish, and claimed
he was an Italian lawyer, up from Roma, with a little pensione
just above the ristorante, where the aroma of pasta
overpowered him. You see me here, he said, entirely surrendered,
as many of us have done over the years. And what was the basis
of our friendship? That we were the only two tables
on an October afternoon in San Gusme? That a few tunes

on the piano, one from their table, one from ours, had sealed
our bond as solidly as a king's ring impressed in wax?
No one was going to the gallows after a final meal. No one
would be betrayed. He wanted my book of poetry, trusting
it would be "a good book, if not *the* Good Book." Why
will I never visit him, never trust him, he who was more
warmly human than my American manners allow?
Why do I sniff a trap where there is no trap? Is there?

C'EST DOMMAGE

C'est dommage. I'm in the tony suburbs.
F. Scott Fitzgerald on a James Merrill grant
to Peggy Guggenheim's chateau west of Paris.
Yes, I've heard of the Muslim problem in the cités of Meaux.
And the miracle of Montreuil's sixty-two langues
and sixty-two ateliers leased for centimes to the latest artists
who have no means. And I know that's where the action is.
But you see, my wife Zelda's studying the bourgeoisie.
And so we simply must live among the natives.
We don't intend to *go* native. No, that would be unthinkable.
But the weather *is* nice here when the sun shines
on their jewels. And the news is nothing but nice news.

Oh, perhaps something happens if one ventures out
to Saint Cyr—not exactly a car-jacking, but one's seats
are stolen, if they're crushed velvet. And some protest's
always within earshot near École Salvador Allende,
and the flics check the train-tracks—for bombs or bums?
Doesn't something happen here in the well-heeled villes,
say, at a raclette for sixteen or an apéritif at eight,
when the cognac is very old and very dear and the host
breaks out his collection of antique trains or confesses
her weakness for signed monographs on Vichy collaborators.
Well, yes, something happens. But is it the thing that needs
to happen? Is it a happening? Or just the passing of time.

There's no way to end this poem responsibly. I know that now.
So let's get soused and revel in what we believe, reveal whatever
we believe we heard between a dozen drinks at the mairie accueil.
That Algerians beaten and drowned in the Seine in October '61
are pure myth. The Nazi occupation never happened. Old Maréchal
Pétain had them fooled. And why not rid the cities of a few Jews?
There's liberté and égalité, said the mayor, and then there's

the immigrant problem. I understand immigration. I'm Parisian,
only by default. My heart's in my terroir, my Alsace pays,
along the Rhine, sweating like a sausage in a simmering pot
of kraut. Follow that river north, straight to the Arab suburbs
east of Paris—and that's where our smokestacks are, plenty
of cheap labor by day and by night the smokestacks rain ash
over their breeding bodies. We wouldn't change a thing.

PLEASANT WEATHER IN CORNWALL

Sticky sea and sand on my hands—
better than blood on them—implicate
me on a leisurely day in 2003
doing nothing for world peace—
on the other bloodless hand,
doing nothing against it, either—
doing nothing but enjoying the bare-ass
babies unembarrassed about peeing
in sea-green pools, bikini-thin
mothers lathering sun-block on their
muscled sons perhaps for the last time
before girlfriends or war take over,

before they enter the cold Cornwall sea—
swimmers, surfers, snorkelers, cloaked
in black-and-red wetsuits like coats
of arms bobbing on an empire
of waves—at the moment
all leisurely and peaceful
in a country awash with blood, I'm afraid,
blood on the front page and back page,
and all the pages in-between, on the hands
of today's news and tomorrow's—
and, yes, yesterday's too—damn
bloody, bloody news not even the sea
can wash off on a fine day.

THREE

Last Friday, in the big light of last Friday night,
We drove home from Cornwall to Hartford, late.

It was not a night blown at a glassworks in Vienna
Or Venice, motionless, gathering time and dust.

Wallace Stevens
"Reality Is an Activity of the Most August Imagination"

There it was, word for word,
The poem that took the place of a mountain.
—Wallace Stevens

(T)RAVEL/UN(T)RAVEL: NORTH WALES, SNOWDON PHILOSOPHY
for Wallace Stevens

Count me one object among many
as I stop to strap on a hood
and jacket, cover a pack, and bend
again into misting rain. An object
passing objects probable as sheep
or stone, possible as gravel fill
or wooden rail, definite as nettle
or thistle, all bearing themselves
out of clouds on Mount Snowdon.
Hiss of steam engine somewhere
above me, low hoot and high
whistle, spoil the milky
silence, until one must wake
(mustn't one?) and believe
something up there exists
as certain as the end of earth
at Snowdon's summit and the
plunge into space, if one wanders
beyond what is sensibly revealed—
if not palpable as an object,
then a piercing sound from a high
invisible place, not quite object,
not void, not song, not human
word, but human made, for certain,
and recorded in the human mind.

L'OPÉRA

How much gold-leaf is there, anyway, in this lively, deadly city,
which threatens to turn all of us to admirers on a frieze?
Dim-sighted from the glint of gold-tipped gates, gold-
plated domes, gold-brushed angels and gargoyles.
And now, the flash of these photographs, gold-toothed
smiles from Chinese tourists who hug my daughter
before the gilded central staircase of L'Opéra
and say, *Dui bu chi. Take photo. Xiexie.*
And snap and flash for whatever guests will come
to their seven-course dinners back in Beijing and say
Hao ji la! to the black-haired host whose face is lit
and framed beside the blonde girl with the gold-sequinned coat.
What does it cover over? The grim line of the mouth
opens on a gold smile when everyone's looking and the flash
captures it. Beneath gold, there's dull metal or pale plaster
or less. But the opera ceiling shimmers when the lights go down
and night fills the enormous space. And out of a hollow, dark throat
come the gold-leafed notes of an aria freezing the others to a tableau vivant.

GRAY BANLIEUE

Gray banlieue in layers of rain, forty days
and nights of rain, from God's watering
can sprinkled across these old Catholic
suburbs, and out to the plains of Versailles,
where I sink down among winter rows
of root crops and broccoli, muddy clay
clasped to my boots, my mood. This mud is

buffer mud, mud that separates St. Cyr
from St. Germaine, separates each churlish,
chichi town. Nothing bas grows
into something haut. Nobody's neighborhood's
deluged with undesirables. I could stamp
the mud off my boots, stumble into town,
where the hedges are green and thick as gates.

I've slipped through those streets many times—
named for composers and poets who, if they were ever
welcomed, nihil obstat, would cast themselves out,
muddying the banlieue's well-kept signs,
scattering the rows of roses as they went,
with a vibrance shaken from genius's scruffy head
that would make them self-respecting again –

I've slipped into many rooms of happy apertif-
sipping French, stared at their muted wall fabrics—
little fuzzy nubs of gray rain sprouting foregrounds
of thick black varnish, Vuillard or Courbet,
Louis Quartoze chairs, Napoleon III sideboards,
and oh, those spreads of patisseries, fromages et du vin,
that would fatten any artist's resolve into drunken loutishness.

Out in the fields surrounding the town, gray rain keeps watering the vast patches of broccoli, keeps thickening the mud buffers. The broccoli heads are stiff with waiting. I'm waiting with them, for some unrepeatable pattern to sprout in their dense heads.

BLUE BANLIEUE

This morning, all the sentences line up.
And behave themselves, don't they?
Two concurrent life-sentences mean
I'll be here awhile in the well-heeled commuter blueness
while the husbands settle down in train cars and office cubicles
and the wives pretty up for mid-morning ménage-a-trois,
circus sex, really, swallowing fire, balancing on a sword—
life-as-you-know-it and its reincarnation. Life, friends, is,
or isn't, boring—so much depends upon half
the women in France (half!) dallying in orgies,
waiting for the skies to clear, le ciel bleu.
Bring in the bluebirds. The white doves. Those
sounds that harmonize the human grunts and groans.
They really are out there, in the sky, the whole menagerie.
These sounds are the best I can do to bring them to you.
Believe it or not—go on, believe it—they're making birdsong
in a blue sky, breaking a string of 28 consecutive soundless gray banlieue days
with a bloody period and exclamation point! What a grand
transition. Mostly, it's the roses, the roses opening
before my eyes can stop them—even when I suppress them
they won't be suppressed. And I have to offer one to you and you and you
in this blue weather. In this blue weather, they push out a foot, if not an inch,
or a hand, and another foot. Once, I closed my eyes to this blushing little world.
Now they're wide open, and the gray weather's disappearing in my beard,
at my temples. It's just the end of one life, the beginning of the next.
Nothing serious. Just the blue sentences lining up perfectly
this morning, just another several lives to live.

ON THE WAY TO THE PANTHEON, CROSSING RUE MOUFFETARD

Algerian lamb on a rack, globes
of grease fall and sizzle and –

three Africans in dashikis, dance the Yankadi
to "Night in Tunisia," blasting out the door of Tout Le Jazz and—

next door, the patisserie. Mais d'abord—first, first, line
up, faites la queue, as all proper Frenchmen must, lined,

framed, encadré, preferably light-complected, but égalité
is in order here, and—*Bonjour, monsieur,*

quelle pâtisserie désirez-vous? the haut one breathes
through her pinched nose, ignoring the brilliantly

blue-black men lounging against the counter.
I can't take it—la religieuse et l'opera et l'éclair—

and still decide to live another year—in this pale body—
trapped on a narrow regime, of lasting—

outlasting those (things) I pass by, bypass, Bombay incense, prajna,
padhama, dhyana, nirvana all curry favor, curry flavor—

because there's just too much—conga,
temple bell, and acidic guitar pulsing my temples—

too much ethnicity etched into my eye, too many
images burning the circuitry—Morrocan break-

dancers and dog shit and Muslims in green jump suits
sucking it up with enormous nozzles—lamb on a rack and globes

of Corsican onions and it's clear I won't make it—
bells of Saint Etienne du Mont, the muftah wailing

from the minaret of the Mosque de Paris, time for—
prayer shawls, prayer mats for the knees, and

this bright mélange on the cobbled streets
confounding the eye, confusing the tongue—

something tight in my throat, these small lanes, lines I have to—
navigate to find my way to the famous dead of Le Panthéon.

PUNTING ON THE CAM

How many ghosts in this river
crowded with punts? Chaucer passed here,
Marlowe, Milton, Herbert, Dryden, Wordsworth, Byron
Coleridge, Tennyson, Smart, Gray—nearly half
the voices of English literature floated
here in their green years over the water
and under the shade trees, already self-possessed,
already swimming in the literary currents of their day.

Today, so many punters on the Cam crowd them out—
rowdy punks out in full force, unschooled
in river etiquette, shout, curse, bump and
tumble out of boats. Even the skilled ones,
Cambridge students on summer break, poling
tourists downstream, pointing out a patch
of grass where Marlowe sat, or scratched
initials on a tree that might be Byron's—

even these students can't parse the rumors
from the facts, the pranks of old poets who postured
here as wildly as those now shimmering in light.
Did Byron keep a bear in his bedroom?
Was Marlowe the Queen's spy? Did Milton defy
the Gardner by planting a mulberry?
Did Wordsworth succumb "to the weakness
of the hour," drunk with wine, stealing

into Milton's old quarters? Was Dryden punished
for disobedience? Did Gray never get a degree,
though he spent most of his life here? Hard to hear
above the hubbub on the river. The ghosts won't speak
above a whisper. So I ferry over to the dust-
quiet library of Christopher Wren and burn
daylight, poring over words penned in their own hands—

as if the scribbling wrist still hung above
the ink—the flourishes of Milton's script
undercut accounts of his tight ill-treatment by the prefects;
the rough-hewn scrawl of Wordsworth's *Prelude* point
his way to a Nature far from scholarly Cambridge;
Coleridge's loose missives, heavy with debt, opium and women,
enlist him in the 15th Light Dragoons
under the name Silas Tomkin Comberbache,
to be discharged under the insanity clause;

Dryden's scraggly signature forecasts disobedience
to the vice-master *for which I have been put out of commons
and gated for a fortnight;* and Marlowe's cramped hand carves
letters wrapped in enigma—*Quod me nutruit, me destruit*—
what nourishes me destroys me—put that
in your pipes and smoke it, or at least, learn it,
young rowdies on these waters—and lastly,
the neat, bold script of Byron's letters

belies his bad-boy image. How calculated
his Byronic shirt, open to the chest, how scripted
his stance, verse, quips and circus bear –
oh, how much like you, youth, posturing
over the water before you fall in and drown,
or float around the next green bend, under the old
willows, and vanish from sight, just a voice
calling back upstream from an ever-widening distance.

LUSH LIFE

Withered heart, in a briar patch
long past rose season you take your ease.
The climate of continual bloom
offends you. Like Wallace Stevens
casting off hibiscus and bougainvillea
for the cold, mental climate of Hartford
assurances, you've prepared to meet your
pacemaker. Has the cold soil of New England
hardened your arteries this quickly,
constricted the bloodflow to veins
that throb at the skin's surface?

Your body's here in the Marquesas. Like it
or not, look out through the portals
of your soul—or sense—
tiare, white love flower,
and the beating hearts of hibiscus
would whisper in your ears.
Or listen to the rooster's reveille
mark his spot in the cross-hatched
sunlight, watch his red coxcomb rattle,
his auburn throat stretch for the force
that will issue from his tropical heart.

Here, the damn birds even fly!—
as do their brooding hens—
up into pandanus and breadfruit trees,
up into coconut and corasol,
to rest their smug bottoms
in the evening's cooling breeze.
It's a kind of safety.
But I have watched the island boys
raise bamboo poles at night

and tip them from their perch.
Then down, down they fall, perhaps

in a wild crowing dream, before the abrupt
neck-snap and toss into the dinner sack.
I hope there are assurances in hen-heaven
greater than the wishing bone, hope
their plucked plumage is restored
for a flight over the feathered town.
—But just now I must return
to earth where a handsome cock mounts
a struggling hen, and just after
the flapping stops I hear nothing
but my pen scratching its undertakings.

DUZI

(Taklamakan Desert, China)

Seven hours of irritable, ass-hard, desert bus ride,
Uighur and Kazakh squabbling with Han, yellow bilious light
glaring from the Taklamakan, from their eyes—finally, the hot wind
withers us into fitful sleep. The Han
beside me dozes on my shoulder, the Uighur
in front flops back on the bench-seat,
his body slipped between my legs, the Kazakh
behind me slumps forward snoozing
between my shoulder blades, and the American
woman beside me, my dear Kate, doubles up
in a painful ball. *Duzi.*
                    No bathroom
on this bus. No rest stop. No tree, bush, or rock.
Somewhere out there lies Turpan, the lowest oasis
on earth, a salt pan of scorching heat, where rain evaporates
before it falls. Yet grape trellises line the streets,
cool shade along the Silk Road. What's the secret?
Snowmelt hundreds of miles off in the Tian Shan,
brought down by ancient irrigation—
each bickering tribe hand-digging its portion
beneath the sand so that water flows
in dark channels all the way to the market town.

But that green swath is hours off. Something
must be done here in the withering moment. I wake
the Uighur and whisper *Duzi.* And point to my wife.
He nods and whispers to the one in front of him,
and on it goes, nodding and whispering, until the last one
shouts to the driver, *Duzi,* and the whole bus shakes,
and skids to a stop. Kate scampers out, up over a low dune,
a second, and third, and squats.

Now the men lean out windows,
others climb to the roof for the best view, and all laugh and clap
each other on the back, Kazakh and Uighur and Han,
to see Kate's white butt above a sand dune, and green
explosions watering the desert, until a cheer
goes up and seeds the few wisps of clouds. Kate wipes up,
a roll of toilet paper like a white bunny tail, and again
men laugh and cheer. I give up, give in,
from anger, to good humor, and cheer my red-
faced wife, the blood far up in her cheeks, the eyes dazzled
desert blue, the taut mouth, suddenly relaxing
into the bawdy camaraderie.

Hao dùo le. Better. Feel better,
they all say. And the bus rolls into rain
that makes the desert bloom and cools tempers
all the way to the wine-crazed town of Turpan.

AMONG THE BAI PEOPLE,

there is a saying:
Every step northward gains the height
of one egg. Where people gauge the world
in egg measures, women rule the roost.
Here, women take one man as provider,
many lovers for pleasure, and
live with their mothers.

Creation myths scored in picture script
are read by the sexless dongbas, only a handful
left. After that, who will read the story
of their beginning? *Stone plus woman*
equals boulder. Stone plus man equals
pebble. Who will remember
the roots of power?

Already, Bai men adopt Chinese ways:
bossing women in the fields, bottoms up,
heads bent to the soil.
Men lead them south to north, rolling the last
potatoes from winter earth, scything the last
winter wheat. Yoked
to their waterbuffalo, men bust
sod, prepare the mud paddies.
Their women bend and plant each slip
of rice. And each step northward earns them
the height of an egg they have forgotten.

2

Each step I take gains the height of an egg.
The Jade Dragon Peaks tower 18,000 feet
above me, dotted, I imagine, with a necklace of Tibetan
lamaseries where monks illuminate scripture

on the prayer wheels and plant bright flags
along the crenellated ridges. In my mind's eye,
I can see the four gated entrance to the heavenly city
where Buddha awaits the journeying mind. Up that high,
above the valley ginkgoes and camellia,
a monkish quiet will prevail.

                When I arrive
at the first temple, dilapidated prayer flags
droop in noon heat. The monks
have long fled. Now four women bustle
me into their kitchen for a meal of eggs,
bin bin and green tea, babbling in broken
Chinese a few revelations: they are Bai women,
dongbas and preservers. More eggs and green tea,
then they lead me to their garden apiaries
where female worker-bees gather nectar,
make honey, maintain the hive, defend it
with ragged stingers that tear
their own bodies open as they sting.
Dongbas click their tongues at the stingless
male drones who do no work, make no honey,
and live a short season to serve the queen.

3

At least an egg, I think, as I descend
from the northern himalayas. Each step
draws closer to Bai women scything the last
winter wheat fields, unearthing the last
winter potatoes. Each step draws closer
to their evening meal of bridge noodles
and hot peppers where the men shout
for more sesame oil, more piju and Dynasty wine,
and the women pass the bottle, bend and smile.

FOUR

You are aware of the great barrier in the path of an American writer. He is read, if at all, in preference to the combined and established wit of the world. I say established; for it is with literature as with law or empire—an established name is an estate in tenure, or a throne in possession. Besides, one might suppose that books, like their authors, improve by travel—their having crossed the seas is, with us, so great a distinction. Our antiquaries abandon time for distance; our very fops glance from the binding to the bottom of the title-page, where the mystic characters which spell London, Paris, or Genoa, are precisely so many letters of recommendation.

Edgar Allan Poe
from "Letter to B—"

Of all melancholy topics, what, according to the universal *understanding of mankind, is the most melancholy? Death . . . when it most closely allies itself to Beauty.*

—Edgar Allan Poe

(T)RAVEL/UN(T)RAVEL: EQUATOR DAZE
for Edgar Allan Poe

Uneventful days full
of waking reveries.
My life is going
nowhere. The great im-
mobility. No desire
to fall toward blowsy
youth and slip inside its care-
lessness, though I do so daily.
And little impetus
to sow the frowzy
rows of futurity, though
I do so daily.
I dally in the idle
sun that works the earth green
whether it wants to or no.
I float in the blue bay
that works up a wave merely
by arching a yawn
and rolling along.
Equatorial air,
simply because it is
there, impedes a bird's friction-
less flight. I breathe it, with-
out parallel, this in-
defatigable light.

MID-OCTOBER, VERSAILLES PARK

From the Gate of Saint Antoine to the Grand Canal
I crush a mile of spiky chestnut husks on cobblestone.
I traipse, amble, double back on piles of yellow
chestnut leaves, still crisp, that need a good cracking
on this muffled, mid-day, mid-week walk within the walls
of Versailles Park. I kick the brown chestnut fruit
burst from the husk, kick it straight into the sheep-shit
pasture of Marie Antoinette and feel I've rattled the order
of these straight corridors and sculpted trees supervising
the eye toward ornate fountains and the Grand Canal's
long shimmering cruciform. I love the fierce resistance
of the sun, how it damages what it must leave, weakening
toward winter. Yes, I'm aging, too, but still kicking
and scuffing my shoes, as the avenues take me straight
to the center of power. Over the long, crossed artifice,
I see the perfect symmetry of the Sun King's chateau,
now shorn of artificial hair and sun-emblems. Opposite,
rows of coiffured trees, shaped in pale rectangles, lead the eye,
doggedly, toward trained horizons. Resistance. Resist. Blink
fiercely till eyes tear, then notice how the trompe l'oeil vistas
slur cock-eyed. Look back now, toward Louis's palace; sun
shimmers on water, shatters it in blinding pointilles; wind tousles
the sculpted trees. With my scuffed shoes, I kick the leaves again.

AUBADE WEST OF PARIS
(January 29)

Joyeux anniversaire, tired one. Sleep denied you
last night as snow fell and stuck and
your separation from the icy biestings
of the cosmos came back to you. Not *now*—
but that first morning—when they lifted
you out like an ice drop from a passing comet
and warmed you into this world—already
nothing was left but vapor in a vessel. Now
dawn's gift of whiteness—a scrim mumming
the lawns and ice spinning cars lazily
out of control—presents itself. Unusual fashion
for this snowless place, like an arctic ermine

wrapped around a model's throat, her body arched
months ahead, birthing styles for the next April
in Paris. This new year the brumal ground's
sealed up. You always wondered how it felt.
Now you know, as sensation sinks deeper in you.
The sky's mute, the ground tomb-hard.
Your heart still beats. Your puffy eyes open.
Below frost line's the warmest place at dawn.

Get dressed, and get to your mumbly place,
your mantic writing table. Thaw, or no
thaw, there's work going on underground.
That old American in Paris, Henry James,
figured it out, he and Strether muttering
the recompense for aging: we feel more deeply
than we do in youth. I didn't know until now he meant
the surface cells froze and died, that we had to dig—
bang that surface with something hard as a metal shovel
to make sparks fly, then dig deeper until the cut
trickles with something wet and warm, and deeper still
until we're into the guts of the thing, down where it lives.

BY THE BARD'S WATERS

Waiting
by the banks of the Avon
near evening, water like beaten silver—
a simile rippling too easily
across my mind, reflecting—what?—
an old carp at feeding time,
orange-going-white with age,
hauling its pack of parasites
to surface and touching
the place where two worlds
meet with his lips—mind reflecting
all it has read of subterfuge and speeches
sotto voce, and sotted Falstaff spitting
Good night, sweet prince into the wind,
deus ex machina and human machinations,
cruel Iago, gentle Clarence, and Hamlet's rapier
wit, dagger after dagger, the thrust
of the play spoken to a candle
in the skull, soon to be snuffed out—
until not one uncontrived thought, plot,
surfaces from my muddied head
this typically English gray
day except to say Shakespeare
said it of course elegantly,
brazenly, most foul and most high,
once and for all, that we shall die—
all the waters take us there,
the punts and ferries gliding over
beaten water—clouds hammered
to translucence, to the thinnest
tint of metal, now all afire—
the hordes on shore wander

dully along, stare at fish-ripples
or toss crusts to ducks.
Old, old trees of merry
England—Shakespeare's mulberry,
Beowulf's oak, Anonymous's maple—
all rooted here, holding on
as long as they can, rooted
in the only reality, and yet—
this shimmer of water is
another world, isn't it, perfect
or imperfect as the mind makes it,
shaded by trees, glister of water
that is beaten, unbeaten—
his bald head, his beard and curled whiskers
surface face up in the Avon,
and is that now a smile, sneer,
or censorious frown
where his mouth ripples and a fish
breathes rings of watery salutation
into the living stream—I'm still
waiting.

That skull had a tongue in it, and could sing once.
—*Hamlet,* William Shakespeare

PHYSICIAN IN THE DARK
(Hall's Croft, Stratford-on-Avon, autumn, 1616)

John Hall swirls the urine
in a glass then assays what he sees—
fire and air, choler and melancholy,
Jupiter and Mercury, all out of balance—
so the patient must be bled,
a mixture of marjoram, nightshade,
ageratum, and toadstool concocted,
swirled in a glass beaker over blue flame—
for this patient is important—yes,
every patient is so, but so impatient
for a cure, and John Hall knows enough
to know he's working in the dark—
for hasn't his colleague Harvey
just turned the world on its head
with his theory of the blood's
circulation, so now bleeding a patient
with a straight lancet might belie
the very health of the circle
blood makes in its journey
through the body—this moment,
there's nothing to be done
about what we don't know—
this moment, John Hall's patient
is dying beneath his hands
and will be dead, in any event,
before Harvey or that Dutchman
refines his lenses sufficiently
to see what he has been saying

is an invisible world—
a world to which we all go
at our ends, in any case,
mutters John Hall—as he turns
to his patient, his own wife's
father, her dear William, who knows—
and now, almost, *knew*—more than most men
what the good physician knows
every mortal day of his profession—
that skull had a tongue in it, and could sing once.

BIOGRAPHERS

    (The Borderlands, Northumbria)

Young men should be biographers—
when they can perch at the feet
of a world-class wit,
let his words cinch
around their necks,
until the trapdoor
of character
drops open,
and they're hung
on every word.

          •

Old men should be biographers—
when they've arrived at the borders
of world-class winds, and words
fray against the indifferent distances.

          •

The young man would shine his subject
with a warm enthusiasm—Swinburne, say,
among the purple heather of Northumbria
on a late summer day, madcapping
with his grandfather along the Penine Way,
charging up the Cheviot Hills, and cackling
at how close the billowy clouds are
to the craggy tor—how close
to Hadrian's Wall, all time held
here in an England that goes back
and goes on to time without end—
and Swinburne, yes, "mad Swinburne,"
with his shocks of red hair falling

at right angles from his commanding
head, shouting poetry, profanity, drunken
brilliance to the circling winds that he shall live
forever in men's minds—before the moderns
dismantled him, word by rosy word,
to a minor disturbance in the weather
of English literature . . .

       •

The old man would cast one suspect eye
on the singer, singing like a bird in heather,
cast another cold eye on Northumbrian hills
rolling into the distances, and assess
his twittering words against the wind's
monotone over limestone, throw cold
water on his steamy intrigues, discern
the romantic excess that drifts away
in mist, rinse the chapters of character-
making in a bracing solvent, distil all
rosy gaiety and gray sobriety, all terror
and aspiration, into a single equation
of longing on earth—and have done with it.

VINCENT, AT SAINT PAUL'S SANITARIUM, SAINT REMY DE PROVENCE

If I'm quiet in my room I lie
on the straw mattress with a brown wool
blanket, and my fingers feel the cool iron
that underlies it. I watch the simple walls
of pale yellow that the sun does nothing to,
the honey-colored chair that holds my blue
pile of clothes, the faded red easy-chair
for the doctor, with those unraveling threads
that begin to glint, oh, around mid-afternoon –
Then, I must take my easel and go out,
against all good advice, and use the sun
as I can—for how else to get perspective
on light and shadow, on the line between
garden and lawn in the foreground, wall
and olive trees beyond, and farther off,
those alpilles, those little alps, limestone white.
If they existed alone—but yellow wheat agitates
the plains, waves of green cypress protest
horizontalness, stretching far up the sides
of white hills, pointing mocking fingers
at an always-blue sky that mimics eternity
or somewhere. Beyond it all, the white windy slopes
of Mount Venteux. After that, almost nothing
can take the paintbrush from my hand,
not the terrible blue sky, not mistral light
punishing the stones to wind-scoured skulls
and pock-marked sockets—but if
it becomes impossible for me, I must go
to that other room, across the hall from mine,
where metal tubs the size of sarcophagi
are fitted with dull wooden tops, fitted perfectly
but for two holes—for my head and feet—

a sort of horizontal pillory—but not altogether
unpleasant. For I am soothed by the warm
bath waters, tucked in, bibbed,
by this long wooden "smock,"
with my head on a platter at one end
and my scaly toes waving vertically
in the distance. Then—the unpleasant
splash of ice-water on my brain—a shock
to my mind so complete, it shakes
the sun from my eyes, blackens the blue
sky to a starless night, and completes me
with a colorless towel thrown over my head
until I stop shivering and am
dry and without perspective.

GIVERNY

Old man, I'm almost ready to join you
in the lily pond with the Asian green bridges,
the towering willows waving soft green hair
over the water, the walkways hedged with
orange asters, blue cosmos, yellow daffodils,
pink and purple mallow, blue morning glory,
and another hundred shades of pale cream to neon red—
all color set against a green backdrop of leaves and shade
by which these small bodies take their luster.
I'm not blind to the fact my green body's growing
darker as it breaks down and all the little blossoms
wither. Oh Monet, did you walk out aching
one morning from your red chateau and simply begin?
Two towering trees here, green pears and apples there,
and the rest planted in rows of flowers proliferating
against green fronds, all bending toward a stream
turned by human hands to flood a hand-dug pond.
Did you already picture the signs: this way
to the water lilies, that way to the limed pit.
Or did you turn your back on all future plans
and trudge happily down the thronging paths
of flowers opening that very morning, easy
with your canvas and easel under an arm,
and set up under the willowy atelier, as if
a woman's hair were always whispering
beside your ear, as the light you desired,
lived by, knew as close as anything
to an abiding presence, began to dim,
and the lilies slow-blinking
their great dewy eyes from morning to evening
must be seized upon and set down as color
moving through the hours. And they never,

as far as you could see, complained of
the coming and going of light.
They just opened as far as they could
each morning and prepared to close
when they sensed it was time to close.

FIVE

America is another name for opportunity. Our whole history appears like a last effort of divine providence on behalf of the human race.

Ralph Waldo Emerson, from *America*

The locus of divinity is precisely inside each of us.
—Ralph Waldo Emerson

(T)RAVEL/UN(T)RAVEL: THE WORLD GOES AWAY
for Ralph Waldo Emerson

When I travel, the world goes away.

The tour books disintegrate—
The Insider's Guide, The Outsider's Guide—
mystifications made of last year's desires and copyrights.

(I prefer shambling into the Sistine Chapel:
Why is everyone looking at the ceiling?
And then—the astounding discovery!)

The familiar voice on the audio tour
is no longer Peter O'Toole in the Vatican
or Peter Ustinov in the Forbidden City—

but my own voice so shallow
it's the flat report from an Etruscan cistern,
so deep it's the long black echo
from the wells of Karez.

I couldn't go farther into darkness
if I dug to China, if I took the red-eye
flight to winter in Longyearbyen.

I couldn't go farther toward light
if I scaled the Tian Shan. Travel is the Voice
in the Void, the I's passport to Thou.

WHITBY ABBEY

She heard him singing in the fields,
singing in English to his unruly sheep
who had wandered too far
up the purple-heather vale,
this poor shepherd named Caedmon,
and she went to him and took him
to the simple abbey that was hers
and gave him the simple task of conversion—
to transform his English singing
for a different flock, a foundering
violent group who needed the high
flown Latin hymns brought down
to their vulgar tongue but brought down
beautifully so as to raise up vulgarity
and show its native beauty. And Caedmon,
who had not a word of liturgical Latin
to his name, learned it all, the hymns
and parables and highest laws, and changed
it all to language shepherds loved in the dirty
crowded towns and wind-scoured tors,
English hymns worth remembering, poems
decent as prayers, first versions
of how luscious the language of slaughter
and conquest could sound when the blood
had dried, when the words were converted
to a higher purpose. And she,
whom Caedmon served, who served, no doubt,
as muse, second to none, not even
unto the god of Apocalypse, she dreamed
no more of snakes plaguing the abbey,
nor of Normans invading the coast,
nor of the massive Gothic arches to come,

nor of the final plunder and fire. She packed away
her staff, the one she had used to scatter
the last invasion of vermin, and wrote
her first letter in a peaceable Anglo hand
to report to the venerable Bede—
the rough speech of the fields
was at last converted to singing.

WUYI MOUNTAIN CAVE

At the cave mouth,
our guide said, "A god and goddess
lived happily here under the sun.
When Darkness discovered this,
it covered the sky with stone.
But the gods, with their passion,
pried a slit of light open
and to this day, it gleams
through a ceiling crack, lifting
the spirits of those who pass through."
I was bored with myth—each cliff
or cave resembled another Chinese dragon
or human form fashioned from some golden time.
I was hungry for hard science, precise
terms in my mouth—*calcite, stalagmite*—
to temper the ancient wonder.

But there was only the Chinese guide,
speaking through an interpreter,
"This trip is not for the fearful.
It requires half an hour, a steep climb
up crumbling steps of sandstone, wet
underfoot and wet overhead, and just
a crack of light to squeeze through.
Now we will study the Chinese cliff poems
for strength." And I turned to the ancient
characters carved high overhead on sheer
rock walls. Waterfalls sprayed a curtain
of mist in the air, and behind it, T'ang poems
preserved in red and ochre. I couldn't read a word.
But far off, I could see stone steps carved
into the mountainside, and thousands of Chinese

pilgrims ascending to the ancient temples,
moving vertebrae on an endless spine.

Four of us entered the cave slit
and five minutes into darkness
we were soaked and scraped
with wet clay and limewater. The crack
narrowed to the size of a small child's
frame, and the light above seemed no larger
than an infant's fist. Another slippery minute,
and I heard myself gasp: "Does it get narrower
than this?" "No, worst moment," said the guide
and translator, their voices strained through mist
and limewater falling on my fontanel.

Twenty minutes we gasped for air.
A woman whimpered behind me,
a man whistled ahead of me.
And then the fault line widened,
the seam stretched and delivered us
in twos from the cave mouth. Air
seemed to rush into my lungs. As we stumbled
out of the darkness, there were others
awaiting us, laughing and applauding
our blood clay coloring. And I did feel

returned to the world, the poems on Wuyi
Mountain freshly scrawled above me,
like prophecies on the living, the dead,
and the newly returned.

GHOST TALK

In the tropics it took a while to believe
anything: that cocks crowing two,
three, four, five in the morning
helped to hatch the light;
that winged beings, smudged particles
torn from the light, hovered over me
each night feeding in the blood-shallows
of my arms before they floated off.

It took a while to believe
I would leave these islands
and later, after I had lost myself
to the puaka dance and joined the mad
Marquesan chants in the Catholic church
with a baptismal font made of dolmens
and an altar of bamboo spears,
I believed we preceded the false

cock's cries and would ourselves revert
to Old Ones floating over tohuas all night
until the dogs' mad yapping drove us
from the sky and allowed the sun to rise.
For here in the Marquesas, you understand,
the tupapa'u are black
and, like ghosts everywhere, rattle
their troubles, arriving in a clamor

of palm fronds, departing with the thunk
of a coconut. And whether their tale's
of smallpox, syphilis, impotence,
or the machete's sting
through a jealous heart,
they're still the same

debris of dissolving souls
that smudge the light.

I believe now they enter
the tiare flower each morning
to alight behind the lover's ear
and whisper bloody murder.
I believe they enter the purple
flowers of banana and infuse them
with off-color thoughts so that
a woman, easing the white fruit

from its yellow sheath, commits pau heke
each morning over coffee.
I have come to these beliefs slowly,
have uttered them to no one, until now,
dear readers who float over these troubled
pages like winged congregations in need of blood.
Who am I, you ask. The last frere
eaten in 1914? Not necessarily,

but a ghost nevertheless now that
I've laid me down here
and waited for the shoulder-tap
that never came. I was the one
with his eyes blanched
from staring out to sea. It took a while
to believe I would escape this place
and finally come home to you.

IF I HAVE TO DIE, AND I HAVE TO—

I liked the dress rehearsal, coasting on the high
hills of Volterra: a moving land, a land of waves.
One caught my mind and pushed it to the crest
of a great vantage, where sun splashed
on the long foreground of my life: stark
contours of northern elevations
where I had learned to hunker down,
cramp under cold outcrops, immobilize
myself to stone and snow. Suffused now
in amber light, I felt the cypress taking hold
of what had been: unforgiving, windswept
places, yielding scrub, scree and gradually unbreathable
air. Now walled cities glowed yellow
on every grassy rise. My mind—saved,
this late, from utter exposure! Waves
of forest canopy swaying deep green,
siena soil, wheat rippling blond,
and the palest green grasses waving, washing
my eyes in water colors. The high road to Volterra
opened in every direction on harrowed soil,

                          then leveled itself
along Viale del Ponti, the long promenade
through old Etruscan gates and into town.
But before I could enter, I turned
to scour the Colli Metallifera a final time,
for the one clue: how these metal-bearing hills
that had made the swords were now broken
into ploughshares. I turned again
and went into town, a straggler and dreamer
among the locals tossing bocchi and lazing

on benches. I disturbed nothing, I tell you,
not the 600 urns of Etruscans, not medieval washtubs
scoured to mother of pearl and catching rain in courtyards,
not Torre del Porcellino with the wild boar
carved high up in bas relief, harrowing
saints from some higher place, driving them
downward, toward the earth. For I was tired
of high, windswept places where life demanded
dwarfed fir or mossed rock, orange lichen
digesting stone at the rate of one crumb per millennium.

I was ready for amber light and fertile hills—
but nothing too rich, too high: I preferred the plain
wooden Christ set low in the duomo of Volterra.
Not marble piazzas and porticos, not
glorianna arches and inlaid buttresses,
as elsewhere in Italy, but this town—
this tilled hilltop, suited my mood: for I was
exhausted by the ornaments and opulence
that wealth requires. Exhausted, really,
by Italy, its gloriously constructed past.
Exhausted, too, by the old stark choice
of northern elevations, chiaroscuros
of dark and light. And now this—
this fluid, amber light that drove the eye
from rise to rise and back to earth,
crowned—if crowned at all—by waves
of low olive or pale grasses, here
and there, a glint of the old metal-
bearing minerals, and the punctuated
no, or *yes,* of an upthrust cypress.

THE BENEDICTINE ABBEY AT MONTE OLIVETO

Who is that looking out at us from a third floor window,
smiling slightly, raising a hand, as if in benediction?
Who am I kidding? He knows why we've come: to glom
on to each brick of this mountain fastness on a cypress-
whipping day, to squeeze inside and squeeze the silence
out of silence, smuggle it down the spiraling road to our home.
Impossible, his smile says, hand to his lips. We've come

near closing time, to seal the little cell of solitude around us,
gaze at chapel frescos of the trials and temptations
of Saint Benedict—women with tits thinly veiled behind lace,
bare-assed men diving and splashing in a pond, lots of wine
and gourmandizing around a lavish, supercilious bunch. Whose
raised eyebrow is that, looking out from this crowd of temptresses,
the only one bold enough to look us in the face? Now we know:

one of those unbelievers, Sodoma or Signorelli, whose art
was anonymous. The trick was this: to slip his likeness
somewhere among the seated or standing crowd, the only one
looking out at the viewers looking in—a very early form
of reflexive art—asking what we desire. And what did
he desire—a seat in the sensuous palace, or some quiet,
sunlit studio, with his palette and canvas and model?

Here he is, trapped in his contract with the Church. Monks desired
the tits and ass, the oily leers, painted over, painted out.
But later painters are always restoring the body to its prominence
under the sun, and so, the tits and ass are painted in again. What
do *I* desire? Silence or the banquet stuffed with figs and laughter?
Do I want these details—fleshy breasts and bursting codpiece,
flasks of wine and fruit pressed between a boar's tusks—

or the wind blowing fast outside, making the trees genuflect?
If God is in the details, they're all here on the face of the painting.
But if we love these places of retreat, the old unsettling feeling returns:
even as the eyes graze a painting or monkish cell, we require another place,
solitary, inside us, that just might be bricked up for good.
Who's left inside, looking out with a critical eye, mocking, inviting,
as the world goes by? What master does he serve?

When we walk outside, down the path to the car, the devotion
bell is ringing. There's low, far-off singing, no one at the window.

SIENA

After you climb the four hundred steps to Torre del Mangia
and peer down from the belltower onto the scallop shaped
Il Campo where hundreds of tourists sprawl across the piazza
and hundreds more bend under green umbrellas to nibble biscotti
and sip caffe, and the air's suffused with golden aureoles,
you'll know why swallows double loop the campanile and circle
the nearby duomo, circle all afternoon without coming
down through shafts of Tuscan sun like a knife
and intercession between light's source and its deliverance
to the brick streets below. You'll know why the Council of Nine,
a level headed, merchant lot, launched their earthly plans:
commanded tones of raw and burnt sienna for their houses,
umber for the city walls, and quarried colored marble
from nearby hills for the various facades, flat bands
of pink and green that paralleled the world below.
And puzzle pieced beneath the pilgrims' feet black and white
inlays of marble, Sibyls and Allegories that spoke simply
for the divine mystery. Magnificence, yes. But earthly works
to praise Him and to weight men's passions for the sky with marble
edifices. Today, it's all brilliant and dead as Jesus in his tomb
despite the Gothic arches, the golden stars of apse and dome,
the soaring nave, the pulpit carved of porphyry, the striking
bronze of Saint John, the famous *Maesta* with Mary serenely
poised between saints and angels—no, I tell you, up here,
four hundred steps to the belltower is as close as you come
to the light those ancient ones beheld, and still you must shield
your eyes from the milling ones below, vendors of gelato and vino,
crowds videocamming the hundred diversions of the square's
halved circle. Or else, go down to ground level and pass through
the duomo's bronzed doors and down her arching corridors
and slip into the Libreria Piccolomini where the books

of Pope Pius rest behind glass, and inhale the quiet
that companions books everywhere, like a body and shadow,
a hand and its gesture, an incarnation and its insubstantiation,
and press your palms against the case that keeps you from those
illuminated words scrived by monks whose faith was timeless
and who therefore worked on a scale of time we no longer recognize.
And witness next the margins of the page, eccentric figures
half man, half horse riding with bow bent to the hunt,
or monkeys cavorting with virgins, and know the original
confusion of impulses, the first fires in the blood
that lit a light too high and too charged for reverence
or serenity. And know that even from these familiar
desires you are cut off. Then, when you are ready, turn
to the Three Graces in the room's center, that Roman 3rd-century copy
of a copy, pining for the Hellenic original, the longing
for pastness so strong it comes through each delicate, straining line
of the Graces' arms and legs, even the stumps, the severed, lost, smashed
limbs that strove as far as they could for a prophecy, a fate,
that reached *backwards* to a shared origin. Then return
to the courtyard and stand among the hordes of schoolchildren
with their frazzled, diligent teachers, among the shepherded
tour groups with their staff wielding leaders, among the many
and the few in need of instruction, and witness the uncompleted
floor plan of the duomo's second phase, a few grand arches,
a staircase leading skyward, a few bold walls, the plans
for grand expansion cut short by the Plague of 1348
that cut short half the lives of Siena—65,000 bodies struck
from their souls and piled high in Il Campo, stinking
under the burnt siennese sun—and cut short
their commerce and their fleet and standing army,
and converted them to an annex of Visconti or Medici powers,
and thenceforth, to a beautiful but inconsequential
city on a hilltop, and thenceforward, to a walled museum
whose every medieval scrap and stone was ordained

to be left as is, so others might climb the four hundred steps
of the campanile and behold the swallows slicing through
these shafts of light that fall on the passions below
and illuminate all that grand architecture framed in time.

"Marquesas," "Following in the Footsteps of Melville," Lush Life," "Ghost Talk":
The Marquesas, a group of six inhabited islands in the South Pacific, form a
remote part of French Polynesia. Their language is one of several Polynesian
languages including Hawaiian, Tahitian, and Maori. "Pae pae" and "tohua," stone
sites elevated above the tropical growth, were used by the ancient Marquesan
culture, the former as foundation sites for their bamboo and thatch homes, the
latter as vast sites for their social gatherings, dances, and religious ceremonies.
The "puaka" dance, or pig-dance, is based on one of the ceremonial dances of
the ancient Marquesan culture; "tupapa'o" are Marquesan ghosts; "pau heke" is a
double entendre meaning "go down" and has a distinctly sexual flavor to it. After
the French conquered the Marquesas in the mid-nineteenth century, the islanders
converted to Catholicism.

"Among the Bai People,":
The Bai are one of several minority peoples living in the southwestern provinces of
mainland China. "Dongba" is the Bai word for shaman. "Bin bin" is the Chinese
word for one of their staples, cornbread, and "piju" is the Chinese word for beer.